IMAGES
of America

CAMPBELL COUNTY

IMAGES
of America

CAMPBELL COUNTY

The Campbell County Historical Society

ARCADIA
PUBLISHING

Copyright © 2012 by The Campbell County Historical Society
ISBN 978-1-5316-6253-0

Published by Arcadia Publishing
Charleston, South Carolina

Library of Congress Control Number: 2011944791

For all general information, please contact Arcadia Publishing:
Telephone 843-853-2070
Fax 843-853-0044
E-mail sales@arcadiapublishing.com
For customer service and orders:
Toll-Free 1-888-313-2665

Visit us on the Internet at www.arcadiapublishing.com

This book is dedicated to those who embrace our passion for sharing and preserving images, facts, and stories of our area's history. It is our hope that this compilation will encourage our readers to pull out their photographs and home movies, their collections of articles and documents, and their storehouse of family lore and memories and share them with others.

CONTENTS

ACKNOWLEDGMENTS

If it takes a village to raise a child, it takes a whole county to compile a book such as this. The idea for participating in the Images of America series grew out of a collection of photographs held by the Campbell County Historical Society from our participation in a Department of Historic Resources survey of historic structures in Campbell County. Those photographs launched our project, but we needed far more images to fill a book. People from all over the county have been gracious in sharing their photographs with us. Many of you gave us far more time than we expected or deserved. We have striven for accuracy in our attribution of photographs in the courtesy lines, but if we have confused any names and photographs or information, we ask for your forgiveness. We welcome corrections. Some photographs were unable to be used because of poor reproduction or incomplete information. In addition to the attributions given in the courtesy lines, we want to thank Judy Campbell; Patty D. Doss; Douglas K. Harvey, director of the Lynchburg Museum System; Friends of New London, Inc.; Dan Witt and the Town of Altavista; R. Gene Smith; David Laurell and the administration of Campbell County; and Chuck Bradner with Jones Memorial Library. A special thanks is extended to Virginia C. Colbert and Tim Wilson with the Willie Hodges Booth Museum of the Staunton River Historical Society, who provided the cover photo, as well as many other images. Amelia A. Talley generously gave up many hours to assist us. Her editing skills and her knowledge of Campbell County helped bring the book to its final form. A very special thanks is due Brinkley Gary, acquisitions editor with Arcadia Publishing. You have been so very patient with our questions and concerns. Many thanks to all who had any part in bringing this book from concept to reality. We feel that we have made many new friends whom we hope to see again, but we promise not to again take over your office spaces or kitchen tables with our scanner and laptop.

We invite the reader to learn more about the Campbell County Historical Society by visiting its website at www.campbellcountyvahistoricalsociety.org.

Many, many thanks to the Book Committee:

Barbara Hammock Caldwell

Revely B. Carwile, Jr.

Barbara Hall Keys

Robert M. Merryman

Mary Walker Gough, editor

INTRODUCTION

Campbell County, settled in 1736 and formed in 1781, is located in Virginia's south-central Piedmont region, in the foothills of the Blue Ridge Mountains. The area is rich in both natural beauty and history. Campbell County was named for Gen. William Campbell, the Revolutionary War hero famous for his leadership in defeating the Tories and Loyalists at the Battle of King's Mountain in the Carolinas.

Scotch-Irish Presbyterians first settled in Campbell County in the late 1730s, forming the Hat Creek community. Other colonies soon followed near Flat Creek/Otter River and Concord, and the county grew quickly during the next few years.

In 1757, John Lynch, son of one of the first Quaker families, initiated a ferry service across the James River, around which the present city of Lynchburg developed. Meanwhile, Lynch's brother, Charles, developed Green Level (now Avoca), located in present-day Altavista. Jeremiah Rust donated 50 acres of land in 1784 to create the county seat of Rustburg. Lynchburg was officially created from Campbell County land in 1786. Brookneal, a busy intersection of trails on the Staunton River, was founded in 1802. Altavista was planned in 1907 by a group of businessmen who realized its potential as a strategic railroad location.

In its publications, the administration of Campbell County introduces our county thusly: "Our county has grown and changed with the times without losing touch with its earliest roots. As we proceed through the 21st century, the County continues to offer a compelling blend of history, natural beauty, culture, and economic opportunity."

In 1754, Bedford County was carved from portions of Lunenberg County (formerly Brunswick County) and Albemarle County (formerly Goochland County). The *New Campbell County Chronicles* notes that most of Bedford's members of the House of Burgesses from 1754 to 1775 were from the section of Bedford County that would become Campbell County. William Callaway Sr., William Callaway Jr., Samuel Hairston, Charles Lynch, and John Talbot were the representatives from this area.

William Calloway Sr. gave land for a central Bedford County seat, "New London Towne," in 1754. Lots were laid off in half-acres to be sold by lottery "for one pound, one shilling, eight pence." The homes were required to be 20 feet by 16 feet "within one year after purchase and a brick or stone chimney within four years." The courthouse also had stipulations, to "have a fireplace in each room . . . with six glass windows, brick underpinning . . . the remaining floor is brick and tile."

By 1740, William and Richard Callaway had patented lands along Buffalo Creek at the intersection of Native American trading paths and established a mill and a store. The Callaways led militia forces during the French and Indian War, including the forts at Blackwater and at Anthony's on Otter River. New London hosted the courthouse, jail, stores, ordinaries, a growing number of houses, and the regular militia musters. The Glebe for Russell Parish was established nearby. By 1775, a colonial arsenal supplied gunpowder, cartridges, accoutrements, and repairs to muskets.

In 1781, an act of the newly-established Virginia state legislature provided for the formation of a new county. Patrick Henry recommended it be called Campbell after his heroic brother-in-law, Gen. William Campbell, and it was incorporated on January 1, 1782. New London would be in the new county but would no longer be a central location, meaning a new county seat had to be found.

Campbell courts first met at Micajah Terrell's and then at Micajah Moorman's, which was thought to have been in the area of present-day Route 29 (Lawyers Road). Then, Jeremiah Rust offered 50 acres of land for the county seat. The offer was met with disdain by some who said that Moorman's land—and not Rust's—was "well situated for timber and Good water in the greatest Plenty and is well accommodated with a good Publick house." Rust's meadowland apparently did not offer such amenities, as another petition stated that "there is neither Necessities nor Conveniences . . . Pray that an act may pass your honorable house for Court House to be in the center of county or erected at Moorman's where it now Sits."

However, the majority ruled. In 1785, Rust's land was accepted, and plans were made "to fix the spot for the courthouse and prison and to employ a surveyor to lay off 10 lotts of one acre each with proper streets, one for the court house and publick building on the north side of Main Street and in the center facing the sun, and the others on each side of the court house on the same side of the main street which is 65 feet wide."

A temporary log courthouse was erected, but it was soon sold "to the highest bidder." The second courthouse burned in 1814, and after its 1817 repair, trustees sold the "bricks, nails, and any lumber remaining from the old facility." The third courthouse, known today as "the historic courthouse," was erected in 1848 at a cost "not to exceed $7,000" with the builder prohibited from using "any portion of the material of the present court house." The keeper of the courthouse was prohibited from showing the "upper rooms to strangers without authorization."

Ongoing animosities between Rust's supporters and others caused some to refuse to call the county seat Rustburg, instead calling it Campbell Court House.

Ross's Iron Works, later Oxford Furnace, supplied iron during the Revolutionary War. Busy intersecting trails on the Staunton River brought a tobacco warehouse to Brookneal in 1799 and led to that town's incorporation in 1802. Turnpikes were built and railroads brought more growth, with communities named Lynch Station, Evington, Winfall, Gladys, and Naruna.

Campbell County became a leading world market for tobacco and its manufactured products: cigarettes, cigars, and chewing tobacco. The local economy was diversified with cotton, gristmills, lumber, mining, and manufacturing. Lynchburg became the second municipality in the United States to offer its citizens public water and gas lighting along its streets. Local businesses opened offices in larger cities and in Europe. Oral tradition maintains that when Queen Victoria learned of the new courthouse in 1848, she directed a fitting judicial chair be sent; it is now in the Historic Courthouse Museum. By 1850, Campbell County, which at the time included Lynchburg, had the second-highest per capita income of any county in the United States.

Over the years, the court system outgrew the 1848 courthouse, but until 2012, many rooms of the old courthouse were used as county offices. A portion of the building is used by the Campbell County Historical Society as a museum. A new courthouse was dedicated in 1991.

It is our hope that through this compilation of images, facts, and stories, our readers will cherish these glimpses into the past, enjoy the stroll down memory lane, and appreciate the need to preserve yesterday's stories for tomorrow's benefit.

One

THE COUNTY AND THE COUNTY SEAT

Campbell County is governed by an elected board of supervisors that, among other things, "oversees the budget, encourages economic growth, sets operational policies, reviews and adopts the County's operational and capital budgets, and generally provides services to promote a better place to live and work for all citizens." A county administrator oversees the day-to-day operations of the county. (Courtesy of Robert A. Caldwell.)

Campbell County was the first Virginia county created after the Revolutionary War. Richard Stith was the county surveyor designated to mark the boundaries of the new county; he was paid for his service with 500 pounds of tobacco. Campbell County was named for Gen. William Campbell, hero of the Battle of King's Mountain in the Revolutionary War. The county seat of Rustburg was also called Campbell Court House. (Courtesy of the Campbell County Historical Society.)

Now used as a law office, this is one of the oldest buildings in Rustburg. Barnett Finch bought the property in 1796, and in 1845, clerk of the court John Alexander bought the building. From 1915 until 1935, Goodman's Store operated out of the building. Robert Russell purchased the structure and renovated it in the style of Colonial Williamsburg, using some materials from the demolished Hay's Chapel. (Courtesy of Campbell County Historical Society.)

This Campbell County courthouse, the third one in Rustburg, was built in 1848, replacing an earlier wooden one. The beauty of its Greek Revival exterior is matched by the beauty of the interior of the courtroom, with ornate plaster medallions on the ceiling and the all-seeing eye behind the judge's bench. Oral tradition holds that the judge's chair was given to the county by Queen Victoria. The wooden fence shown here was later replaced by a low concrete wall. This courthouse was replaced with a new one in 1991. (Courtesy of Jane Douglas Moorman.)

The third courthouse was built on the same site as the old ones. When the new Campbell County courthouse was completed in 1991, space in the old one was allocated for county offices; it is now the home of the Campbell County Historical Society Museum. (Courtesy of Campbell County Historical Society.)

The old jail in Rustburg, now used as an office for the county administration, ended its time as a jail in the late 1940s. The chief deputy and his family lived on the ground floor, and the prisoners' cells were on the second floor. Sometimes the prisoners ate with the family or played cards with them. The upstairs with its steel walls retains the holes into which iron bars were fitted. Chief Deputy Paul W. Phillips and his family were the last to live there. For some years after that, the building was used as the county's school board office. (Courtesy of Campbell County Historical Society.)

The Barricks Hotel was earlier known as the Virginia Hotel. James M. Lawson bought the hotel in 1905, renamed it the Lawson Hotel, and sold it in 1913 to Wilton J. Barricks. The first telephone switchboard in Rustburg was located in the hotel and was operated by Clara B. Barricks. The hotel was known for its delicious meals. The Wells Fargo Bank was later built on this site. (Courtesy of Laverne Snow Tweedy.)

The first bank in Rustburg was established in 1924 as Campbell County Bank, with C.I. Anderson as the first employee. In one story, two masked men came in demanding money. Anderson fired a pistol in the air, and the two men made a quick departure and were later apprehended in North Carolina. When the new bank was built, the old bank building, now demolished, was used by the county. (Courtesy of Campbell County Historical Society.)

Jack's Place was established in the 1940s by Jack Puckett and was one of the few eating places in Rustburg at the time. The restaurant was renowned for its hot dogs. Customers often purchased food from inside and took it outside to their car for the whole family to enjoy. The building shown was torn down and ownership changed; the replacement building suffered fire damage and was demolished in 2011. (Courtesy of Laverne Snow Tweedy.)

At one time, Rustburg had a number of mercantile establishments. The location of the George Mortimer Finch store is believed to have been next to the Fountain Hotel. Finch's store offered its patrons everything from flour to "animal regulators." (Courtesy of John D. Nelson.)

Thomas C. Pugh operated a store and post office out of his home, seen here. His daughter, Lillie Forest Pugh, married George Arthur Coleman, and the house became known as the Coleman House. Coleman built many of the homes in the town, as well as the first Rustburg High School. George A. Coleman and his son, Arthur, owned and operated Rustburg Roller Mill. George A. Coleman was also the last mayor of Rustburg. (Courtesy of Mary Coleman Tweedy.)

Ben and Maynard's was on the main street in Rustburg on the property now occupied by the new courthouse. The building, originally a World War I barracks, was used first in Rustburg as a car dealership. Ben Tweedy and his brother-in-law, Maynard Merryman, operated the grocery store for many years. The store closed in the late 1960s. (Courtesy of Laverne Snow Tweedy.)

One section of this Rustburg house dates to 1885. The additions to the house were built by a local carpenter, Andrew H. Trent Sr. At least five generations of the Trent family have lived in the house. (Courtesy of Campbell County Historical Society.)

This home in Rustburg belonged to Guy Puckett, who operated Rustburg Supply Co., a grocery store next door. Puckett was active in the Central Methodist Church (now Rustburg United Methodist Church). The house was demolished to make room for the Rustburg Fire Department parking lot. (Courtesy of Campbell County Historical Society.)

The construction date of the Nelson House in Rustburg is unknown, but it is believed to have been built as a tobacco factory. In 1877, the "factory lot" was sold to Robert Woodson Withers, who sold it to his son-in-law, Judge Frank Nelson. Tradition holds that Jeremiah Rust, founder of Rustburg, is buried in the eastern yard. The house was demolished for the Food Lion shopping center. (Courtesy of Mary Walker Gough.)

The Woodson House was owned by Campbell County clerk Charles W. Woodson. It was built in the 1920s by George A. Coleman, who built a number of other structures in Rustburg. The house is on Route 501 across from the Rescue Squad building. (Courtesy of Campbell County Historical Society.)

The fire tower in Rustburg served a valuable service before the days of local volunteer fire departments. Among those who staffed the tower and kept a vigilant watch for fires were Howard Carwile, Christine Swart, Shirley Mitchell, Frances Bailey, and Orbah Alexander. It was a favorite summertime activity for town children to hike to the top of the mountain and then up the many steps of the tower to chat with whoever was on duty. The tower, erected in 1934, was sold in 2005 for $782 and dismantled. (Courtesy of Robert A. Caldwell.)

Two

AGRICULTURE

This abandoned reaper at the old David Bennett Tweedy home place is one of many in the county that have been left to the elements. As new equipment was purchased, farmers often left the older equipment at the edge of a field or yard. Many farming implements were given as scrap metal for the war effort during World War II. (Courtesy of Robert A. Caldwell.)

Samuel Franklin Caldwell, Lyle Caldwell, Thomas Martin, and Robert Caldwell are part of a "wood sawing bunch." The wheel or drum on the side of the tractor was a Power Take Off, connected to a belt driving a circular saw on a stand in front of the stationary tractor. This was a great laborsaving device for laying in a good store of wood for the winter, but without safety shields around the belt or saw, it was also dangerous. (Courtesy of Robert A. Caldwell.)

This steam power unit is an Eclipse, manufactured around 1900 in Waynesboro, Pennsylvania, and used at Flat Creek Farm to thresh wheat and complete other tasks. Budge Hall helped operate it in the 1920s and 1930s. He stopped running it after a session when it ran out of water and a bolt burst off the body of the machine, nearly hitting him. (Courtesy of Sara Saunders Hollberg.)

Farmers sometimes supplemented their income with custom sawmilling work for neighbors. The ratio of sawmilling to farming varied with the owner. In the era between using waterpower and internal combustion engines, steam engines were used to power sawmills, threshing machines, and other devices. Here, Glover L. Gough moves his steam traction engine to a new site for a customer sometime before 1920. (Courtesy of Thomas E. Gough.)

Grains had to be preserved across seasons until the next harvests. Cats and traps were used to control the ever-present rodents A granary had bins sealed on the bottom and sides like a box. Farmers had to ensure that the granary roofs were maintained to prevent moisture from ruining the stored grain. Some granaries had locks since grain was a tradable commodity. (Courtesy of Campbell County Historical Society.)

George Winston feeds his horse, Belle, and her mule colts. Mules are a hybrid offspring of a mare and a jackass and are usually sterile. Mules have the reputation of being stubborn but are good draft animals; farmers used them to pull wagons, sleds, and cultivating equipment like plows. (Courtesy of Alice May Winston Tilman.)

This small building on Station Road in Concord is known as the "Lime House." In the 1920s and 1930s, topsoil was taken from farmers' fields and mixed with sand for sand-clay roads. As a bit of payback, the government offered lime for the fields. This building, next to the train tracks, was the repository for the lime. (Courtesy of Mary Walker Gough.)

Making molasses was an annual event on many farms in the county. Seen here is Tom Barnard's molasses-making operation using cane raised by George Winston. Customers took their cane to Barnard, who then took it through the processes to turn it into molasses. Making molasses was a laborious task. Once it became commercially available, few local farmers continued to raise sorghum. (Courtesy of Alice May Winston Tilman.)

Clark Winston used this churning apparatus in the milk house on his father's farm. The family of George Winston churned weekly and took butter to Lynchburg on Saturdays to sell it. Many rural families depended on milk cows for their family needs for income or for trading for other goods at the community market. (Courtesy of Alice May Winston Tilman.)

Tobacco was the major cash crop for Campbell County farmers. The first tobacco market in the county was built in Brookneal in 1800, two years before the town was established. Brookneal has been described as "the town born in a tobacco warehouse," and it soon became the market center for plantations along the Staunton River. (Courtesy of Mary Walker Gough.)

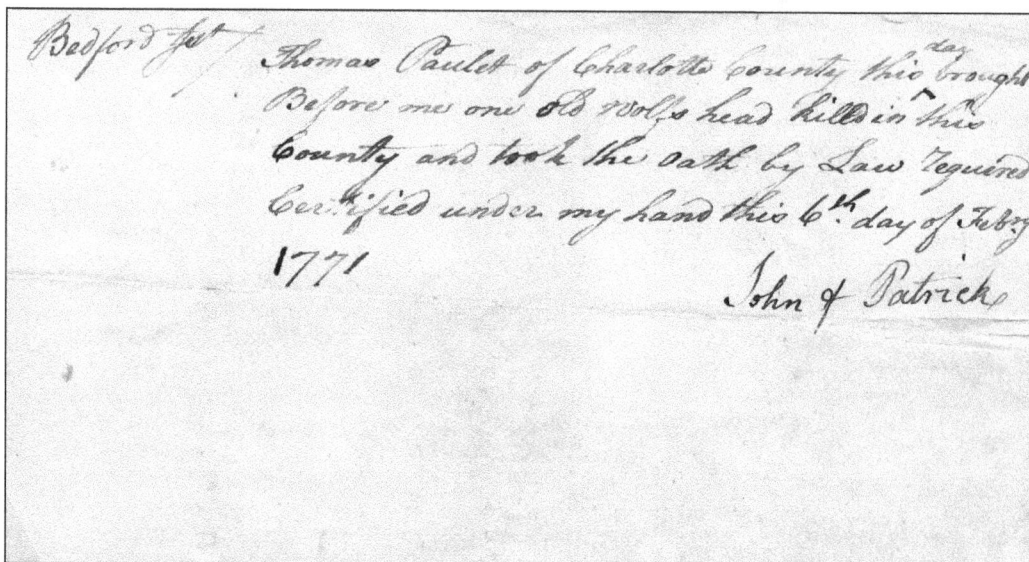

To collect a bounty or to sell furs, trappers often traveled for weeks to the offices of county officials. This 1771 document shows payment made in Bedford County, later Campbell County. Thomas Paulett or his children later moved to the Hat Creek community. John Fitz Patrick of Cedar Forest served as justice of the peace of Bedford County and of Campbell County at its formation and was a juror in the John Hook trial. (Courtesy of Revely B. Carwile Jr.)

The first mill at Bear Creek in the Gladys area was several hundred yards downstream from this site. Bear Creek Mill was sold by Robert Samuel Wheeler to Thomas B. Tweedy in 1905 for $480. Robert Christian Wilkerson operated the mill and is buried in the Wilkerson family cemetery on the property. Wilkerson's tombstone has an etching of Bear Creek Mill. (Courtesy of Robert A. Caldwell.)

Mason's Mill was moved from its original location on Troublesome Creek to the Phillips' farm around 1890. In its first location, the mill was powered by a waterwheel; in its second, it was powered by a steam engine. (Courtesy of Robert Bass Phillips.)

The Red Mill on Route 615 in the Mt. Zion community was built around 1940 and powered by an engine. The Wilkerson family operated this mill, one in Rustburg, and the Bear Creek Mill. When Red House Road was straightened in the 1930s, this lot became separated from James Edward Carwile's field; he used the open space for family reunions. Later, his widow sold it for the mill lot. (Courtesy of Revely B. Carwile Jr.)

Rucker's Mill in Concord was owned by Allen M. Rucker. It was a roller mill that first had a two-stroke gasoline engine and later an electric motor. The mill is located on Station Road in Concord, but, like many county mills, it is no longer in operation. (Courtesy of Mary Walker Gough.)

Built in 1900, the Rustburg Roller Mills was owned and operated by George Arthur Coleman and his son, Arthur Pugh Coleman. The frame structure withstood the ravages of several fires and was in continuous use until it closed in 1964. It was torn down shortly thereafter. A restaurant stands on the former site of the mill at the intersection of Routes 501 and 24. (Courtesy of Mary Coleman Tweedy.)

Spring Mills was built in 1880 by Tom Harvey. The lumber for the mill was sawed with one of the only left-handed saws in the state. The mill had two stones and ground cornmeal and flour, cow and horse feed, and hog and chicken feed. The Harvey family operated the mill until it closed in 1958. In 1996, floodwaters from Hurricane Fran destroyed it. (Courtesy of Gladys Tweedy Martin.)

27

Dr. George Wickliffe, owner of the Wickliffe Mill in Brookneal, was a fascinating early county entrepreneur. In addition to the mill, Dr. Wickliffe invested in real estate, as well as having owned Wickliffe's Big Department Store, a tannery, a printing press, and a tobacco warehouse and factory, among other ventures. He was a medical doctor and a geologist, as well as a fine musician, a dancer, and general Renaissance man. A rather mysterious man, Wickliffe never told from whence he had come to Brookneal. Before his death in 1897, he is reputed to have said, "I have lived a mystery; I will die a mystery." He is buried in the Wickliffe Cemetery in Brookneal. (Courtesy of the Willie Hodges Booth Museum of the Staunton River Historical Society.)

Three

BUSINESS

Bell and Deacon Amoco operated at 3820 Campbell Avenue from 1954 until 1966. Gasoline was about 25¢ a gallon when this photograph was taken for the grand opening. Note the "Free Gifts for All" sign. Prizes included a lawnmower and a bicycle. Widening of Campbell Avenue forced the station to close, but it reopened on Tyreanna Road and continues business as Deacon's Garage. (Courtesy Nancy Blackwell Marion.)

Dallas Allcock, owner of the popular Virginia Inn on Route 29, bought and cured hams and sold them to restaurants all over the area. A fire on the premises threatened the smokehouse, but Allcock wetted down the building and saved it—and the hams—from destruction. (Courtesy of Nancy Allcock Parker.)

The Colonial Restaurant was purchased in 1963 by the Dallas Allcock family, who had previously operated Virginia Inn. By 1965, the Allcocks had also bought the adjacent Colonial Motel. In the early 1970s, the complex was sold to the Allcocks' daughter and son-in-law, Nancy and Morris Parker. The tradition of fine cooking first begun at Virginia Inn continued at the Colonial Restaurant until its closing in 2012. (Courtesy of Nancy Allcock Parker.)

The N.I. Walthall store served the town of Brookneal from the late 1890s until the 1930s. The first N.I. Walthall store was a wood frame one, which burned in the Brookneal fire of 1912. Walthall then built a brick store, which carried an assortment of dry goods and clothing, but it closed as a result of the Great Depression. The building later was occupied by Leggett Department Store. (Courtesy of the Willie Hodges Booth Museum of the Staunton River Historical Society.)

Carson's Store in Concord began in 1930. Owner Ray Carson found that using a barter system drew customers to his store. Carson stocked items from peas to plows, and before long, more space was needed. In 1951, the store relocated to its present location and became "a country store with a convenience store twist." James Carson sold the family store in 1998. (Courtesy of James F. Carson.)

Lewis C. Carter established Carter's Store in 1895. In 1903 he relocated across the street into David Ward's Store. In 1916 Charles L. Carter took over the business from his father. Calvin P. Carter became the third generation Carter to run the store, which carried almost any item the area residents might need. The store ceased operation in 2011. (Courtesy of Adele Tribble Carter.)

This hotel in Altavista was described in a 1909 *Altavista Journal* article as being "an up-to-date hotel, with steam heating and cold water apparatus with fifty guest rooms, expected to be filled by summer visitors." A $50 prize was offered to the public for the winning hotel name and "Commonwealth Hotel" was selected. The hotel was torn down around 1970. (Courtesy of William J. Burgess.)

The Dalton House in Altavista was built in the early 1920s by Andrew J. Dalton, president of the Mountain States Coal Company in Kentucky, at a cost of almost $500,000. The lovely structure boasted 40 rooms, 12 baths, and two showers. Dalton lost his fortune in the Great Depression and sold the estate to the town of Altavista for $35,000. Nothing remains today of the estate. (Courtesy of Robert B. Carpenter Jr.)

The Evington post office, as was customary at the time, had separate entrances for blacks and whites. Whites used the front door; blacks used a side door. Repurposing former post offices into homes or offices was common, as was moving such structures. The one pictured was relocated behind Winston Miles' Store around 1960. (Courtesy of Campbell County Historical Society.)

Foster's Store in the Hat Creek area was also known as Guthrie's Store. It was built and operated by Richard Lawson. Thomas Foster was the next proprietor. The landmark country store served the needs of the community and was sold to Clayton Bryant in 1997. (Courtesy of Virginia Crabtree Colbert.)

Jumbo Restaurant was built in the 1950s by Herman McMaster. It offered drive-in service, but as the sign over the front door indicates, booths were also available inside. Each booth had its own jukebox. The business has changed hands several times and is now within the city limits. Jumbo Restaurant draws especially large crowds for breakfast and Sunday meals. (Courtesy of David Wingfield.)

THE LANE COMPANY, INC., ALTAVISTA, VIRGINIA.   "THE WORLD'S FOREMOST CEDAR CHEST MANUFACTURERS"

The Lane Company, established in Altavista, became a major manufacturer of household furniture with plants all over the country. Production of the renowned Lane Cedar Chests began under the leadership of E.H. Lane Sr. in 1912. Over the years, other plants were acquired and the company produced products ranging from recliners to wartime pine ammunition boxes. The company closed its Altavista plant in 2001 due to foreign competition. (Courtesy of Robert B. Carpenter, Jr.)

The Lawson House, also known as Harvey's Hotel, in Brookneal served the town until its closure in 1964. James Lawson built and operated the hotel and owned a number of businesses in Brookneal. He also served as a postmaster in town. The current town library and the Willie Hodges Booth Museum of the Staunton River Historical Society are now on the site of the demolished hotel. (Courtesy of *The Union Star.*)

Lynch's Tavern, or Ward's Road Inn, was situated nicely to serve as a wayside inn, located on Ward's Ferry Road midway between the Staunton River and the James River at Lynchburg. This mid-1700s gathering place was operated by a Lynch family with no known connections to Lynchburg's founder. The structure went into disrepair and was eventually isolated in a wide median when Route 29 was widened to four lanes, where it crumbled. (Courtesy of Elizabeth Elliott Williams.)

The historic Mead's Tavern in New London, one of the oldest structures in central Virginia, has had a multipurpose existence. It was licensed as an ordinary by Col. William Mead in 1763. Later it was used as a tavern, a hotel, Roland Academy for females from around 1810 to the mid-1820s, a private home, a parsonage for New London Presbyterian Church, a doctor's office, and a private residence. (Courtesy of Revely B. Carwile Jr.)

The Merry Garden near Fairview Heights was a dinner and dance club built around 1932. It also included a swimming pool and bathhouse and a skating rink, which opened in 1948. A cannery for owner Warren Falwell's restaurants operated in the basement of the complex, with a temperature-controlled storage room for potatoes. The complex was razed during the construction of the Route 460 bypass. (Courtesy of Edna "Pee Wee" Falwell Twiddy.)

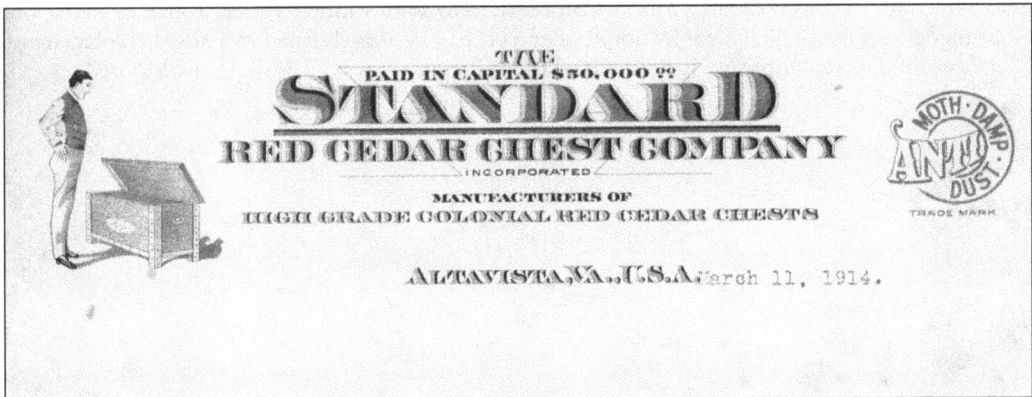

This letterhead serves as a reminder that before there was a Lane Cedar Chest company in Altavista, the business was known as the Standard Red Cedar Chest Company, and it started as a box factory. The company operated under that name from 1912 until 1922, when it was changed to the Lane Company. By 1930, the plant had increased production from 10 chests a day to over 250 chests a day. (Courtesy of John D. Nelson.)

Moore's Country Store on Route 460 began in 1926 as Riverside Service Station with Herman Carter Moore as the owner. In addition to offering four brands of gasoline, Moore sold a variety of goods including coffee he ground himself. In its early days, seen here, the store offered products ranging from tires to Nabisco Biscuits. A cooler held bologna and other groceries needing refrigeration. The name later changed to H.C. Moore's Store, then to W.R. Moore's Store. Today, it is Moore's Country Store, known widely for its hot dogs and chili. The store burned in 1978; its replacement is built around a sycamore tree that survived the blaze. (Courtesy of William R. Moore.)

Allen Tweedy sold appliances in the mid-1930s from his home on Perrow Street (now called Drummer Street) in Rustburg. Later, he built this small brick building on Main Street where he and his son, A.C. (in the driver's seat), sold stoves, refrigerators, and other home appliances. His grandson, Mitch, still operates an appliance store down the street. (Courtesy of Laverne Snow Tweedy.)

The Virginia Inn was a popular dining and lodging place at the intersection of Route 29 and old Route 24. Dallas Allcock built it in 1948 and operated it until 1955, when he sold it to Wilbur Knight. When Route 24 eastbound was rerouted, the building was demolished, taking with it many memories of fine eating. (Courtesy of Nancy Allcock Parker.)

The Vista Theater in Altavista held its grand opening on July 1, 1936, with the feature movie *Private Number* with Loretta Young and Robert Taylor. Built at a cost of $35,000, the theater and balcony had a seating capacity of 685, and the front was described as "modernistic." The theater offered a drinking fountain and "rest rooms for both ladies and gentlemen." (Courtesy of William J. Burgess.)

An early article described the waterworks in Altavista as being "one of the finest water works in the South, and no city or village in the world has finer, purer water. It was so ordered that a never failing stream flows . . . these springs pour forth from mother earth." This may be the only utilitarian facility to be described in such poetic terms. (Courtesy of William J. Burgess.)

The Lynch Station community grew around a station established in 1873 after the Lynchburg and Danville Railroad was completed. The depot was named Clarion to avoid confusion with Lynchburg. From 1884 to 1900, the town was incorporated and became a leading commercial center. Wilkinson's Store was one of the mercantile establishments. (Courtesy of Robert A. Caldwell.)

Col. Edmund Tate purchased lands on Blackwater Creek in 1782 and in 1809, which adjoined the lands of John Lynch. He developed Tate's Springs as a resort, famous for its chalybeate and sulfur mineral waters. A rock-lined path and steps cut into the stone ledges leading those "taking the water" to the series of springs. Colonel Tate died before his plans were fully completed, but his brother and son completed the operations. (Courtesy of Revely B. Carwile Jr.)

A series of mineral springs, each with distinctive stonework, were features of Tate's Springs. In 1828, a group of cottages and a bathroom were constructed. In 1840, commercial operations were stopped after a terrible storm interrupted the work. Tate Springs Farm passed into the Murrell family, and in 1926, was annexed into the city of Lynchburg. Blackwater Creek Park and Lynchburg General Hospital are now nearby. (Courtesy of Revely B. Carwile Jr.)

Mays Variety Store in Brookneal was established in 1926 by Richard G. Mays and his father. Advertisements pronounced Mays Variety Store as the "Leader of Low Prices." The store's best sellers were work clothes and shoes, but a variety of other products were on the shelves, such as tobacco twine, nail polish, and lamp chimneys. This photograph was taken at the store's 50th anniversary celebration in 1976. (Courtesy of the Willie Hodges Booth Museum of the Staunton River Historical Society.)

W.B. Woodson was a businessman who operated a hotel in Concord. The W.B. Woodson lodging was actually a boardinghouse, according to long-time residents. The building now houses apartments. Concord was a leading competitor to become the hub of the Norfolk & Western Railway but lost out to "Big Lick," now known as Roanoke. Had Concord won, the town would be far different from the residential community we know today. (Courtesy of John D. Nelson.)

Brookneal was a tobacco market before it was a town. The town's location along the Staunton River and the area's red clay soil both played a role in Brookneal's rise as a bright tobacco market. This was one of three or four warehouses that at one time boosted the town's economy. (Courtesy of the Willie Hodges Booth Museum of the Staunton River Historical Society.)

The Old Fort Cottage Hotel was opened in 1931 by Carey H. Falwell, who sold the business to his brother, Warren, in 1938. The complex was nestled between the fork of Route 501 and Route 460, a strategic spot for travelers. The field between the two rows of cottages was used for grazing sheep. Falwell used the wool from those sheep for blankets on the hotel's beds. (Courtesy of Edna "Pee Wee" Falwell Twiddy.)

This post office and home of James E. Hughes was in the Yellow Branch community. In 1818, the area was known as "Cross Road on Quarry Branch" and later changed to "Yellow Branch." Nearby was a park used for tabernacle meetings, militia musters, and family reunions. Nearby inns included Lynch's Tavern and Dudley's Tavern. This community is known today for Yellow Branch Elementary School and the Campbell County Vo-Tech Center. (Courtesy of Robert M. Merryman.)

Four

CHURCHES

Grace Episcopal Church was built in 1855 east of Lynchburg in the Mount Athos area. The rounded window and steeple were added later when it was converted to a mission church of St. Paul's Episcopal Church in Lynchburg. Membership declined, and the church was deconsecrated in 1954. Attempts were made to restore the building, but it fell victim to the elements and neglect. (Courtesy of William R. Moore.)

Bethany Methodist Church on Bethany Road near Rustburg grew out of a church school at Long Mountain School. The building was erected at a cost of $625 and was dedicated on July 30, 1899, with 41 charter members. Additions and improvements have been made over the years and the church celebrated its centennial in 1999. (Courtesy of Campbell County Historical Society.)

This lovely edifice, built in 1875, was the second Bethlehem Methodist Church in Concord, the first having been established in 1840. As was customary at the time, a partition inside the church separated the women from the men. It was demolished in the late 1980s when the Methodists bought their present building from the Baptists, who had just built a new church. (Courtesy of Campbell County Historical Society.)

Central Methodist Episcopal South, known today as Rustburg United Methodist Church, was established in 1876. The church history states that after the Civil War, "there was a need for unity of persons with both Union and Confederate sympathies." Note the two doors—the men entered on the right and the women and children on the left. The current brick church was dedicated on May 12, 1958. (Courtesy of Mary Coleman Tweedy.)

The Church of the Good Shepherd near Evington was built in 1871 on land donated by Capt. Fleming Saunders and Evalina Smith, for whom Evington is named. The church, deconsecrated in 1975, continues to be used for special events and burials. Author John Monk Saunders, who was married to actress Faye Wray of *King Kong* fame, is one of the notables buried here. Clark Gable attended Saunders's funeral. (Courtesy of Campbell County Historical Society.)

Early's Chapel United Methodist Church was built in 1874 and was named for Bishop John Early. The church was remodeled twice, and classrooms, restrooms, and central heat were added in 1959. Early's Chapel is part of the Bethany Circuit, with Bethany and Indian Hill United Methodist churches. A church cemetery is on the property, which is at the intersection of Spring Mill Road and Nowlin's Mill Road. (Courtesy of Robert A. Caldwell.)

Evington United Methodist Church was organized in 1879. This building was erected jointly by that congregation and the local Masonic lodge—now known as the Newman Lodge—and was dedicated in 1881. The congregation used the first floor as a place of worship, and the Masons used the second floor for their meeting place. Stained glass windows were dedicated in 1952, replacing the etched windows. (Courtesy of Robert A. Caldwell.)

Hat Creek Presbyterian Church was established at the site of the first settlement in Campbell County in 1742, four years after it was initially settled. William Irvin, the grandson of area founder John Irvin, wrote a history of the church in 1854. The present edifice is the fifth. (Courtesy of Revely B. Carwile Jr.)

Indian Hill United Methodist Church, "the little church on the hill," was established in 1912. An unusual feature of the church is that the floor slants toward the pulpit to provide a good line of vision. Classrooms and a fellowship hall have been added. Local legend has it that Indian mounds are in the area of the church, hence the name. (Courtesy of Campbell County Historical Society.)

This charming frame church, Leesville United Methodist Church, was the first church in the Leesville area and was a sentinel for the community. Adjacent to the sanctuary is a former school building, which now provides classrooms for the church. (Courtesy of Adele Tribble Carter.)

Long Mountain Baptist Church, located off Oxford Furnace Road, was first known as Mount Vernon Baptist Church. A white congregation worshipped there in the morning, and a black congregation held services in the afternoon. In 1874, the church was given to the black congregation and renamed. That building and its school burned down but were rebuilt in 1880. The church shown was built around 1969. (Courtesy of Campbell County Historical Society.)

Mount Hermon Methodist Church was founded in 1825 in the community later known as Lynch Station. Ralph Lee gave the land, John Lee provided logs for the building, and John Early was the first pastor. The log structure was replaced in 1876 by this frame building, which was itself replaced in 1948 by the larger, brick structure still in use. (Courtesy of Alice May Winston Tilman.)

Mount Vernon Baptist Church dates to 1832, when it was located at the foot of Long Mountain. In 1870, a larger church was needed and one was built on present-day Crews Shop Road. The first public school in the Concord area was held at the church. A cemetery is also located on the grounds. (Courtesy of Campbell County Historical Society.)

New London United Methodist Church North, located on Alum Springs Road, served the black community until the late 1980s. This 1930 structure replaced an earlier building on this part of Lot 17, which was deeded by the Thompson family on November 18, 1851. Free blacks and slaves previously held religious services in a brush arbor outside the village. Friends of New London is currently working to acquire the property. (Courtesy of Revely B. Carwile Jr.)

Mount Zion United Methodist Church on Red House Road traces its history to 1825, when a log house of worship was erected on land donated by Micajah and Elizabeth Hubbard. This photograph was taken at a community gathering around 1897. (Courtesy of Janice Bailey Driskill.)

This stately country church on Route 606 near Concord dates to 1835, when some of the members of Old Concord Presbyterian Church established New Concord Presbyterian Church. In 1885, the present church was built by Thomas Harvey, with classrooms added in 1951. The Owen Cheatham Foundation made possible a renovation of the sanctuary and the addition of a steeple, fellowship hall, kitchen, and vestibule. (Courtesy of Campbell County Historical Society.)

The Owen R. Cheatham Memorial Gardens were established at New Concord Presbyterian Church in 1973 as a tribute to Cheatham, who was raised at New Concord Presbyterian and founded Georgia-Pacific. This monolith is the focal point of the garden. (Courtesy of Campbell County Historical Society.)

Otterwood Presbyterian Church on Route 682 was established in 1874 on property donated by Abner and Mary A. Early. According to *Campbell Chronicles*, the Earlys gave land for a church "in consideration of her interest in the cause of religion, and of his interest to promote the moral welfare of the county." Membership declined and services were only held four times a year before the building was eventually given over to another denomination. The Otterwood Presbyterian Church Association maintains the church and its cemetery. (Courtesy of Robert Bass Phillips.)

Perrow's Chapel at Marysville was established around 1885 as a Methodist Episcopal church and is said to have been funded in part by a gift from Queen Victoria. Since 1969, the building has served as a Mennonite church. (Courtesy of Robert M. Merryman.)

Pilot Mountain Baptist Church, located on Route 646, was built about 1899 on land given to the black community by the Cardwell family. The building was modernized in 1992 with the addition of siding, new doors, and a handicapped access ramp. A large cemetery is behind the church. (Courtesy of Campbell County Historical Society.)

South River Meeting House on Fort Avenue was annexed in 1976 by the City of Lynchburg. Sarah Clark Lynch, mother of Lynchburg's founder, John Lynch, gave the land for a log church in 1757. The church held weekly, monthly, and quarterly meetings for Bedford and Campbell Counties. This structure, the third, was built of stone in 1798 and renovated in 1902 as part of Quaker Memorial Presbyterian Church. (Courtesy of Revely B. Carwile Jr.)

This church in Rustburg was built in 1850 to be shared by four denominations. The upper floor was used by the Sons of Temperance, though by 1855, that group ceased to exist. Trinity Episcopal Church purchased the building and shared the space with Mackey Masonic Lodge, which met upstairs. In 1928, it became the Rustburg Presbyterian Church. Over the years, improvements have been made to the structure. (Courtesy of Mary Walker Evans Fletcher.)

Salem Church was founded in 1870 by James Carson and his daughter, Martha Ann Carson. The first building was "a crude structure of wood set on field stones." Its replacement was erected in 1920. Church historian Robert B. Phillips knows of two unusual features at Salem United Methodist Church: "An elevated floor, and an oculus, a small round window traditionally signifying the all-seeing eye of God." (Courtesy of Robert Bass Phillips.)

Silver Grove Baptist Church was built in 1889 and is located "70 feet on Otter River Road," which is now known as Village Highway, in Rustburg. A new building was erected in 1923, and over the years, other improvements have been made, including the addition of a narthex. Since its beginnings, Silver Grove has served the black community of Rustburg. (Courtesy of Campbell County Historical Society.)

White's United Methodist Church, one of the oldest churches in the area, was established as a Methodist Episcopal church in 1812 on two acres of land donated by Robert White and John DePriest. The church, located on English Tavern Road, is especially well known for its "Lord's Festival," based on the practice of farmers donating one acre of their harvest to their church. The church carefully maintains its cemetery. (Courtesy of Mary Walker Gough.)

Martha Jane and Lucy Thomas Callahan, daughters of William Tarry Callahan and Metilda Jane Pribble, tend to the grave of their brother, Carl Fielder Callahan, in this heartbreaking photograph. Carl was killed in an automobile accident at age 24 in 1929. Salem United Methodist Church is in the background. (Courtesy of Barbara Hall Keys.)

Five

HOUSES

This home near Hat Creek, now owned by the Nowlin family, was called Locust Plain Dairy Farm when Louis Clark Asher and his family lived here. Asher married Alberta Elder; their daughters, Julia Iantha Asher and Marian Asher Fawcett, were both historians and genealogists who taught in the local schools. Members of the family are buried in the cemetery beside the families of earlier owners, the Clarks and the Marstons. (Courtesy of Revely B. Carwile Jr.)

This house on the corner of Third Street and Perrow Road was built in 1814 and is said to be the first house built in Altavista. "Aspen Level" is also known as "Preacher Jenks's House." The preacher's brother, Gerard Jenks, sold land that became the town of Lane Siding—now Altavista—in the early 1900s. (Courtesy of the Campbell County Historical Society.)

Avoca, in Altavista, sits on the homesite of Col. Charles Lynch (1736–1796). This house, constructed in 1901, is one of the area's best examples of Queen Anne–style architecture. Dr. Lindley M. Winston donated Avoca to the town of Altavista in honor of his family in 1981. Avoca is listed on the Virginia Historic Landmark Register and in the National Register of Historic Places and operates as Avoca Museum. (Courtesy of Robert A. Caldwell.)

Blenheim, originally called Red Oak, was built by John Reid sometime before 1809, when he sold it to William Jones, son of Maj. Thomas Jones. Jones paid £500 for the house and more than 300 acres. The house retains its original weatherboard and windows and is distinguished by fine, if somewhat provincial, woodwork. Situated along the Falling River, it is listed on the Virginia Historic Landmark Register and in the National Register of Historic Places. (Courtesy of *The Union Star*.)

Caryswood, in Evington, is a fine example of Italianate style and is on the Virginia Register of Historic Places. It was built in 1854 by Maj. Robert Chancellor Saunders and named for his wife, Caryetta Davis. Roberts served as a Confederate officer, a delegate in the General Assembly, a trustee of New London Academy, and superintendent of Campbell County schools. (Courtesy of Sara Saunders Hollberg.)

William Creasy built this home on Three Creeks Road, facing Red House Road, around 1810. The family of Boler Cocke was the next occupant, with a Revolutionary War soldier and War of 1812 officer buried in the family cemetery. The Burks family followed, and, by marriage, ownership passed to the Fray family. During the Great Depression years, the Fray place was over 1,200 acres, and the house shown became a tenant home. The wife of J.J. Fray was born here; he was superintendent of Campbell County Schools from 1921 to 1961. (Courtesy of Revely B. Carwile Jr.)

This cabin from the late 1700s is an example of Federal style/vernacular architecture, which makes use of locally available materials and styles. Located in the Long Island area, it was the home of Daniel M. Black, who married Mildred Rosser, the daughter of Francis Walker, in 1818. The chimney has a brick with the year 1776 etched in it. (Courtesy of Campbell County Historical Society.)

Dr. Richard Hewett's home, Otter Oaks, on Flat Creek, was built on land originally belonging to Col. John Callaway (1738–1821), who served through the Revolutionary War and became Campbell County high sheriff and treasurer in 1785 and a trustee of Lynchburg in 1786. Dr. Hewett (1827–1897) married Frances Dorothea Michie and served as a Confederate surgeon. Barite mines were on the property. (Courtesy of Campbell County Historical Society.)

This charming structure was the home of Dr. James S. Irvine in Evington. The trim along the roofline is also featured on several buildings at his estate, Flat Creek, as well as at his Bedford County home, Burnt Chimney. Dr. Irvine is said to have had the first x-ray machine in the area. (Courtesy of the Campbell County Historical Society and Steven Wood.)

This is believed to have been the first house built in Concord. Built by Robert Wilson for his cousin, Robert Cardwell, the house was located in a field diagonally across from the present-day Bethlehem United Methodist Church. The house was disassembled in the 1990s and moved to Manassas, Virginia. (Courtesy of Gladys Tweedy Martin.)

Green Hill, in the Long Island area, with its more than 5,000 acres, was often described as "the most completely self-sustaining plantation in the county." Samuel Pannill built this brick Georgian structure with round brick columns and an interior of hand-carved woodwork. Although a wealthy man, Pannill stipulated upon his death, at the age of 94 in 1864, that he was to be buried only "in a plain, decent manner." (Courtesy of W. Scott B. Smith.)

The Henry G. Lowry house was also known as the Alice Cox Walton home. Consisting of one and a half stories, the house was built around 1881 and was one of the first properties in the area to be owned by a black family after the Civil War. The property was purchased from Eva S. Smith, for whom Evington was named, and has changed hands over the years. (Courtesy of Campbell County Historical Society.)

Irvindale is the ancestral home of the Hat Creek Irvins. This 1854 house replaced an earlier one destroyed by fire. The "new" Irvindale was built by Creed Clark, a direct descendant of Maj. John Irvin and his wife, Mary Ann, on the site of the former Irvindale. Though in a state of disrepair today, the home reflects the "simple but classic architecture" of the time. (Courtesy of Mary Walker Gough.)

Although known as the Farmer home for almost a century, this farm on Route 691 in the Evington area was previously owned by Norbonne B. "Nob" Thurmond (1827–1906) of Nelson County. His adopted daughter, Mattie, married Albert Farmer, and they lived here with their children. The house, built in 1850, began as a one-story log construction with a separate kitchen and other outbuildings and was expanded and modified over the years. (Courtesy of Campbell County Historical Society.)

This farmhouse, built between 1850 and 1875, may be the second house built in Altavista and was the second home built on the Brooks-Jenks farm. The bricks for the chimney are said to have come from an outbuilding at Aspen Level. Gerard Jenks and his family lived in this house, located across from the current War Memorial Building. (Courtesy of Campbell County Historical Society.)

This house overlooking the James River near Mount Athos was the home of Edward D. Christian. The large home was built on an English basement and had rock foundations. When the home was razed, the foundation rocks were used to create a low wall lining the driveway and around the replacement house. (Courtesy of William R. Moore.)

This is the west side of the Naruna home of John Wray Carwile, who was born about 1781—the son of Jacob Carwile Sr. John Wray Carwile married Martha W. "Patsy" Maddox and raised a large family. He purchased land from the Matthews and Lipscomb families and operated a blacksmith shop a short distance north of this house. This farm location is noted on the 1864 Confederate engineers map of Campbell County. (Courtesy of Revely B. Carwile Jr.)

The Haden home, located on Route 24 in Evington, is believed to have been built around 1890. Dr. Charles Watts Haden was the son of Leonidas and Athea Arnold Haden. The elder Haden ran the Haden and Bragg Sawmill in Evington. Dr. Haden married Kitty Langhorne, and in 1912, set up a medical practice in his parents' home. Later his office was in the front yard of the home. Dr. Haden was a well-loved and highly respected physician. (Courtesy of Campbell County Historical Society.)

The Hix Farm, also known as Long Mountain Farm, was built in 1804 on what is now Oxford Furnace Road and was once a stagecoach inn. It has been in the Hix family since 1863, when it was deeded to Bettie Gough Hix in the will of her father, William A. Gough. The oldest part had slave quarters in the basement, and there is a slave graveyard on the property. (Courtesy of Campbell County Historical Society and John Bell, Esquire.)

Plain Dealing, on Epson's Road near Brookneal, was built around 1795 by Capt. Robert Cobbs, who married Ann G. Poindexter. Cobbs donated an acre of land nearby for a religious meetinghouse to be used by all denominations. One of their sons, William Cobbs, purchased Thomas Jefferson's Poplar Forest. Plain Dealing is known now as the McIvor Place. (Courtesy of Virginia Crabtree Colbert.)

Sen. Carter Glass operated Monsview Dairy Farm on Candler's Mountain, where he maintained a herd of purebred Jersey cattle. He was a son of Maj. Robert Henry Glass and Elizabeth Christian and was a brother of educator Edward Christian Glass. This home and farmland were located in the City Farm area and are now owned by Liberty University. (Courtesy of Revely B. Carwile Jr.)

New Glasgow, in the Leesville area, was the home of Col. James Callaway, who played a significant role in Bedford and Campbell County history, leading the Bedford Militia in the Revolutionary War. When Campbell County was formed in 1782, he was appointed county lieutenant, the highest office in the county at that time. In 1789, Colonel Callaway built Royal Forest in Bedford County and died there in 1809. (Courtesy of Campbell County Historical Society.)

Nick-Up is believed to be the oldest brick house in the county and has been called "one of the best examples of the early taverns in this vicinity." Richard Stith, the first surveyor of Campbell County, was one of its owners, and Patrick Henry is said to have been a guest in the tavern as he traveled between his Red Hill and Long Island estates. (Courtesy of *The Union Star*.)

Oakdale, in the Gladys area, was built in 1820 by Capt. Adam Clement, who fought in the Revolutionary War and was later the county sheriff. Tradition holds that the father of Samuel Langhorne Clement/Clemens—Mark Twain—was born in this home, though the accuracy of that is not known. Clement's son, Maj. Adam Clement Jr. (1826–1915) lived here and was a state senator and county sheriff. A Clement family graveyard is on the grounds. (Courtesy of *The Union Star*.)

This lovely home on Route 757 off Oxford Furnace Road was built in 1890 by the Diuguid family and is said to retain its original weatherboarding. A Diuguid graveyard is on the property. In 1983, the Daughters of the American Revolution placed a plaque at the base of the grave of George Diuguid (1762–1838) commemorating his service in the Revolutionary War. His wife, Nancy Sampson Diuguid, is also buried there. (Courtesy of Campbell County Historical Society.)

This humble building in Brookneal was the birthplace of Lt. Gen. Lewis Andrew Pick, who engineered the 1,030-mile Ledo Road, a major supply line for American and Chinese troops in the China-Burma-India Theater in World War II. Critics said that the road "couldn't be done," but Pick completed it. Generalissimo Chiang Kai-shek named the road the "Stillwell Road" in honor of General Stillwell, but Pick's engineers referred to it as "Pick's Pike." (Courtesy of Willie Hodges Booth Museum, The Staunton River Historical Society.)

This home, built by Confederate major Robert Chancellor Saunders, is situated across from the Church of the Good Shepherd in Evington and served as its rectory. The last rector to live there was Rev. C.C. Randolph. One of the Reverend's daughters, Bessie, served as president of Hollins College. Mr. and Mrs. E.B. Hughes bought the building in 1924 and lived there for many years. A plaque in the horse stable read "Holy Nag." (Courtesy of Campbell County Historical Society.)

Depending on the spelling, Rees, Reese, or Rhys Evans (1719–1813) emigrated from Wales to Chester County, Pennsylvania, in 1752, and then to the Concord area with his wife, Bridgett, at least two sons, and several brothers and cousins two years later. The trunk he brought from Wales rests inside New Concord Presbyterian Church, slightly west of his homesite. His grandson, Reese Evans, born in 1783, was a militia captain and father of Maj. Daniel J. Evans. (Courtesy of Campbell County Historical Society.)

In the Evington area, Rick-o-hoc—one of various spellings—was built by William Hickson in 1871. The name is said to have come from the novel *Ivanhoe*. Later, Rick-o-hoc became the home of the late state senator William Irvine. Senator Irvine was a farmer and a mine operator who built a bomb shelter in the hillside near his home. This house is no longer standing. (Courtesy of Campbell County Historical Society.)

This stately home on Red House Road is believed to have been built by the Rice family around 1810. Later, the Williams family lived there, and for many years now, it has been in the Driskill family. There was a small office in the yard, which served as the Mt. Zion post office from 1841 to about 1862. This area was also known as Rowdy. (Courtesy of Mary Walker Gough.)

Campbell County has a number of houses called the Rock House. This one in the Gladys area is shown in a state of neglect, but it stands as a sentry and today is in a good state of repair. The walls of the 1790 house are three feet thick, and the interior is noted for its woodwork, which is said to have been carved by Hessian soldiers. Nathaniel Payne is the first known owner, followed by John Alexander in 1828. When his daughter, Olivia Alexander, inherited the property in 1837, the estate consisted of many outbuildings and over 1,200 acres of land. (Courtesy of Virginia Crabtree Colbert.)

Robert Richardson Cardwell (1844–1922) and his wife, Sallie Kate Wright (1848–1940), lived in the area between Route 24 and Bethany Church Road in a house he built. Cardwell was a farmer and had a sawmill. In his youth, he walked to work at Oxford Furnace before serving four years in the 2nd Virginia Cavalry. His daughter, Marian Cardwell Tweedy, lived many of her 106 years here. (Courtesy of Gladys Tweedy Martin.)

Shady Grove, on Route 850 in the Gladys area, was built around 1825 for Paulina Cabell Henry, daughter of Dr. George Cabell of Point of Honor in Lynchburg. It has been said that Paulina Cabell Henry was trying to emulate some of the architectural details found in her father's home, and Shady Grove is considered a fine example of provincial Federal architecture. A Henry family graveyard is on the property. (Courtesy of Campbell County Historical Society.)

The James Moreland Tanner House, located off Route 751 in the Gladys area, is of wattle and daub construction and is considered to be "an excellent example of ancient English building techniques." The original owner's name is unknown, but the house is shown on Civil War maps, and perhaps was given to Tanner and his wife, the former Jane Asher, by her father, John Asher. After imprisonment during the Civil War, Tanner was found dead on the courthouse steps in Rustburg, presumably from war wounds. (Courtesy of Campbell County Historical Society.)

The original part of the Thornhill-Kirkland house in Concord was a log structure built in 1870 by Dr. George W. Thornhill. Over the years, two wings and an enclosed porch were added. The original one-piece staircase is still intact. It has been said that the rain falling on the west side of the road in front of this house, along Route 24, runs into the James River, but that water on the east side runs into the Roanoke River and on down to North Carolina's Albermarle Sound. (Courtesy of Campbell County Historical Society.)

Viewmont on Moon Mountain was built by Littleberry "Berry" Moon on property acquired from William and Sarah Early Anderson. The house reportedly had a widow's walk, which is very unusual for central Virginia, and a second-floor balcony, both of which have been removed. Diane Popek writes in *Tracks Along the Staunton* about the "fire boy" sleeping in front of one of the fireplaces in this house. When he awoke from the cold, he knew it was time to stoke the fire. (Courtesy of Campbell County Historical Society.)

The county has at least two estates named Walnut Hill. This Walnut Hill, on Lawyer's Road, includes an original section built between 1796 and 1802. The property was given to Judith Clark as a wedding gift from her father when she married Samuel Moorman in 1796. At that time, the property consisted of 5,000 acres. The home remains in the same family. (Courtesy of Campbell County Historical Society.)

The middle portion of this house is the oldest and dates to the 1700s. It was built by the Webber family and then occupied by the father of W.H. Burruss, who was the founder of Burruss Land and Lumber. In 1868, it was acquired by John Pleasant Arthur, whose mill was on the east side of Flat Creek. The two oldest portions of the house are constructed of logs covered with weatherboarding. (Courtesy of Derek Arthur.)

White Hall, built in 1810 by John S. Payne, is located about 1.5 miles east of Long Island on the Staunton River. Payne named his home after his grandfather's home in Goochland County. The home is known for its weaving house that contained spinning wheels, flax wheels, and looms. One of John Payne's daughters, Blanche, married Col. Robert Woodson Withers, circuit court clerk. (Courtesy of *The Union Star.*)

The Watts cabin near the Flat Creek community, built between 1790 and 1820, has original Federal mantle and trim inside and unusual triple sash windows. In 1796, this tract was conveyed from Christopher Irvine to Sgt. William Watts, a veteran of the French and Indian War and a delegate to the Constitutional Convention of Virginia in 1776. It later passed to Judge Fleming Saunders and his wife, Alice Watts Saunders. Boxley Materials Corporation currently owns the property. (Courtesy of Sara Saunders Hollberg.)

William Watts purchased lands on both sides of Flat Creek in 1796. He died less than two years later, but his widow, Mary Scott Watts, outlived him by nearly 40 years. Their daughter, Alice, and her husband, Fleming Saunders expanded this house, Flat Creek, in the 1830s. It burned down in 1981, but the property is still owned by Watts-Saunders descendants. (Courtesy of Sara Saunders Hollberg.)

This structure was built between 1828 and 1847 as a duplex slave quarters on the Flat Creek farm of Judge Fleming Saunders. It is composed of two cribs, corner-notched and joined together with a massive fieldstone central chimney. This building became a doctor's office and exam room after Dr. James Sinkler Irvine married Evie Saunders, granddaughter of Judge Saunders. This porch faces the original Courthouse Road. (Courtesy of Sara Saunders Hollberg.)

This image of the Flat Creek farm duplex quarters and office of Dr. James Sinkler Irvine details the techniques to notch and join the corners. The bottom log, or sill, is over 40 feet long. Directly to the rear are the log smokehouse of the same era and the sites of the kitchen and the Flat Creek mansion house (both burned in the 1980s). There are numerous smaller outbuildings. (Courtesy of Sara Saunders Hollberg.)

Six

PEOPLE

Extended family members pose at a reunion of descendants of Thomas Hill Wooding and Olivia Ford Gilliam held at Landover, the home of Dr. Glover D. Gilliam and Eliza Bolling Jones, near Naruna in the late 1940s. The children of Dr. and Mrs. Gilliam were Martha V., Eloise G., James R., Eliza B., Olivia F., Walter F., Emma J., and Thomas W. (Courtesy of Elizabeth Stone Byers Potter.)

Brookneal's Volunteer Fire Department was established in the 1940s. The men wear dress clothes for this photo opportunity. From its early days, they were first responders to calls in areas beyond Brookneal and represented the volunteer spirit of America at its best. (Courtesy of Willie Hodges Booth Museum of the Staunton River Historical Society.)

Lt. Gen. Lewis Andrew Pick was born in Brookneal in 1890, the son of George W. and Annie Crouch Pick. The family moved to Rustburg for the boys to attend school there. Lewis was an athlete at Virginia Polytechnic Institute (VPI)—now Virginia Tech—and his brother, Charles, was a major league baseball player. Lewis was the chief engineer for the China-Burma-India road, and in 1949, he became chief of the US Army Corps of Engineers. Lieutenant General Pick died on December 2, 1956. (Courtesy of Willie Hodges Booth Museum of The Staunton River Historical Society.)

The late Brandon Stone, a graduate of Virginia Tech, is shown here with a representative of *Farm Journal* magazine. Stone raised a variety of crops and livestock on his farm in Campbell County. In this issue, he was featured for his innovative method of egg collecting. Brandon and his brother, Paul, were best known as the first farmers to produce hybrid corn on a commercial basis. (Courtesy of Elizabeth Stone Byers Potter.)

Calvin Coolidge Moon was the first black Marine drafted for World War II from Campbell County. Praised for his skill as a sharpshooter, Moon was promoted to the rank of corporal and was honorably discharged in 1946. He died in 2010 and was buried with military rites at Hat Creek Baptist Church in Brookneal. (Courtesy of the family of Calvin Moon.)

The Alexander family cemetery was located on the former Cedar Hills Golf Course. Because of quarry expansion operations conducted by Boxley Materials Company, seven Civil War–era graves were moved in 2007 to White's United Methodist Church. Surviving members of the Alexander, Nash, and Moorman families, as well as Civil War reenactment groups, gathered for a memorial service. Carter Elliott Jr., a descendant of the Alexander family, is shown speaking at the ceremony. (Courtesy of Alice May Winston Tilman.)

This gathering was held in the fall of 2011 to celebrate the reopening of the G.H. Jones Store in Sherwill. Audrey and Ann Scott Cardwell are the owners of "Uncle Glover's Store" and offer activities at the store on most Sundays in the spring, summer, and fall. The band Deja Moo is shown playing. (Courtesy of Mary Walker Gough.)

The Concord Fourth of July Parade was started in the 1960s by the Concord Ruritan Club. Tractors, scout groups, church floats, Shriners, political candidates, and vintage cars all make this parade a favorite event for area citizens, and it attracts spectators from other locales as well. Thomas Evans (Uncle Sam) poses with Mary Lantz Maiden, who comes yearly from Richmond to enjoy the festivities. (Courtesy of Mary Walker Gough.)

This photograph was taken on Church Street on the day Company B, National Guard, mobilized into federal service, marched past Monument Terrace and through downtown, and entrained for war. The soldiers, including then-sergeant Samuel R. Gay Jr., were from Lynchburg, Campbell, Bedford, and Amherst Counties. Company A, "The Bedford Boys," spearheaded the first assault wave onto Omaha Beach on D-Day, suffering heavy causalities. Company B comprised the second wave, to reinforce A, but navigational error caused their assault boats to land a half-mile distant, on a less-defended section. Company B fought through Normandy, the Battle of the Bulge, and Germany. During training, Sergeant Gay, who eventually obtained the rank of major general, volunteered to be an officer of Nisei-Japanese-Americans in Italy with the 442nd Combat Infantry, the highest-decorated American unit of World War II. Leading is Capt. John R. Pugh; second rank is Lt. Dewey Taylor, and beside him is Sergeant Gay. Major General Gay died in 2005. (Courtesy of Phyllis Oppleman Gay.)

Earl Calohan Sr. will always be remembered for providing fresh turkeys for Thanksgiving and Christmas tables. He began his turkey farm in 1923 with 20 turkeys. Calohan was introduced to poultry raising when he married Marion Arthur, who brought some chickens into the marriage. After Earl Sr. retired, his son, Earl Jr., took over his business and today, David Cardwell, Earl Sr.'s great-grandson, runs it. (Courtesy of Nina Calohan Thomas.)

Lawrence and Calvin Falwell enjoy playing with an animal seldom seen in central Virginia. In 1931, a circus caravan broke down across from the present-day Falwell Airport. The elephant pushed the van uphill so that it could then roll downhill to Warren Falwell's Shop. During the week of repairs on the van, the elephant lived in the Falwell yard, to the fascination of the Falwell children. (Courtesy of Edna "Pee Wee" Falwell Twiddy.)

Maude Garbee (1885–1971), George Winston (1884–1951), and their 13 children posed for this photograph at Lone Oak Farm in 1928. They are, from left to right, Robert, Mattie, Bowling, Cabell, Louise, Eleanor, Clark, Annie, Alexander, Etta, Charles, Ernest, Maude (holding Alice May), and George. (Courtesy of Alice May Winston Tilman.)

Margaret Franklin's image is seen here, affixed to convex glass. She came from the large Franklin family of Concord, Pilot Mountain, and Sherwill. In 1749, Lewis Franklin patented 850 acres on the headwaters of Falling River, followed by Owen Franklin in 1773 and 1788 and Edmund in 1780. Owen and Edmund Franklin were ensigns in the Revolutionary War and Robert and Thomas Franklin also served. (Courtesy of Revely B. Carwile Jr.)

Fay Moorman and her sister, Mary Moorman, were beloved citizens of Campbell County. Miss Fay, a clerk for many years with the Campbell County School Board, captured her memories of growing up in the 1890s on the family farm, Rock Brook, in her book, My Heart Turns Back. They were the daughters of Thomas and Wortley Crawley Moorman. (Courtesy of Mary Walker Gough.)

May Garbee Bell is seen here in 1971 at age 95, just before riding her horse in a parade in Rustburg. The wife of Robert K. Bell, May was known for her stamina and work ethic. Taking care of livestock came as naturally to her as doing domestic chores. May was a beloved member of a large extended family. (Courtesy of Alice May Winston Tilman.)

Rustburg families gathered for this group photograph in 1897 on the courthouse green. The old board fence surrounding the courthouse green is visible, as is the Virginia Hotel—later called Lawson Hotel and Barricks Hotel—and a sign for the Fountain Hotel. The photograph includes members of the Nelson, Withers, Petty, Finch, Spriggs, Gettle, Callaham, Bruce, Pugh, Goggin, Coleman, and Rosser families. (Courtesy of Patty Wilburn Bent.)

The Nelson house in Rustburg was a favorite gathering place for family and friends. Identified in this picture are Ida Withers Nelson (front center left), holding the youngest Nelson child, also named Ida Withers Nelson. Judge Frank Nelson (seated front center right) is holding their son, William. (Courtesy of John D. Nelson.)

Before the days of television, local ball teams received great public support. This is the 1947 Patrick Henry ball team featuring, from left to right, (first row) Russell Upshaw, Carlton Carwile, Lawson Mayberry, Atwood Carwile, Ed Evans, and Bill Swart; (second row) Billy Davidson, Tom Phillips, Sonny Merryman, Kenneth Walker, Gilbert Evans, John Davidson, Jim Stone, and Coach Hutch Overbey. (Courtesy of Floyd W. Merryman.)

Paul Younger is a third-generation basket maker, following in the footsteps of his grandfather and mother. Younger fells oak trees and then splits, dries, and cures the lengths before soaking the strips to make them pliable. Most of his medium-size baskets take between 10 and 15 hours for the weaving process alone. He was a participant in the Fall Festival of America at the Smithsonian, representing the best craftsmen in Virginia. He is featured in Law and Taylor's 1991 book, *Appalachian White Oak Basket Making: Handing Down the Basket.* (Courtesy of Paul Younger.)

Leslie "Peggy" Kilgore and her husband, Claude F. Kilgore, gained fame as the creators of the character cornhusk dolls, the "Little Cornhusk People." Claude was responsible for the driftwood bases upon which the dolls stand, as well as making accessories, such as tiny musical instruments, using only natural materials. Mrs. Kilgore died in 2005 and her husband followed in 2006. Both are buried at Hat Creek Presbyterian Church. (Courtesy of Amelia A. Talley.)

When one thinks about Campbell County's eccentric characters, the four Russell sisters often come to mind. Their father, Richard Henri Russell, built a home and storehouse in the 1850s on old Ward's Road—now English Tavern Road. The daughters lived in the home place all their lives. From left to right, they are Mary, Annie, Lollie, and Sydnor Russell. (Courtesy of Alice May Winston Tilman.)

This gathering is believed to have been on the grounds of the tabernacle meeting site at Yellow Branch, where camp meetings and family reunions were often held. The site was favored because of its water source and shade trees. A small building on the grounds became Yellow Branch School and later the home of Dayton and Lena Monroe, who named it Taberna, meaning "a crude place of learning and worship." (Courtesy of Mary Walker Gough.)

This group celebrates the annual Uncle Billy's Day in Altavista. The brainchild of William George Lane Jr., the First Saturday Trade Lot was begun as an outlet for his produce and to generate extra income for his family of 15. The trade lot remains a popular gathering spot for buyers, sellers, and casual lookers. (Courtesy of William J. Burgess.)

Gladys and Alec Moore stand in front of Rock Castle around 1925. Their grandfather, Warren Walker Moore, was the farm manager at Rock Castle, the home of the Alexanders and the Withers. His son, Jackson Warren Moore, married Lutie Ann Brown and was the farm overseer at Shady Grove. Later, he became the farm manager at Red Hill, where they began a family, before returning to Rock Castle. (Courtesy of Billie Newman Carwile.)

Will Henry Newman takes a break from riding around his farm near Otter River. Newman (1864–1953) and his wife, Eugenia Clay Overstreet, had 11 children, including two sets of twins. He purchased the former Capt. James M. Haden place, now known as White Oak Dairy Farm, and sold it to William Payne Phillips in 1920. (Courtesy of Billie Newman Carwile.)

Seven

SCHOOLS

Rustburg High School's first graduating class, taught by principal Charles Poole in 1910, included, from left to right, (first row) Mazie Gettle, Mary Moorman, Lucie Withers, and Fannie Goggin; (Second row) Albert Stone, Lewis Pick, and William Nelson. (Courtesy of Jane D. Moorman.)

The clerical Building.

The General Assembly of Virginia enacted legislation in 1906 to establish and maintain a system of public high schools. The first one in the county, Rustburg High School, opened in September 1906 with 30 students, for a two-year high school program. This white frame structure was built by George A. Coleman. (Courtesy of Jane D. Moorman.)

This brick school in Rustburg, built in 1918, replaced the first high school in the county. In 1928, an addition, also brick, was built with an auditorium, six classrooms, and a shop and cannery in the basement. Today, the old Rustburg High School is a part of Rustburg Middle School. (Courtesy of Campbell County Historical Society.)

The Campbell County Training School began with elementary education in 1921, and by 1927, offered a two-year high school program. It was made possible largely through the tireless efforts of the Rev. Thomas Tweedy and former slave Gabe Hunt. In 1951, when Campbell County High School was erected, this frame building served the black elementary students from the area. In 1957, a new school, Central Elementary School, was opened across the street. (Courtesy of Campbell County Historical Society.)

This early version of Altavista High School was built in 1910. A second floor was added in 1913 for additional classroom space, but fire destroyed the building in 1917. The next year, a brick building was erected, around which the much larger current high school is built. (Courtesy of Adele Tribble Carter.)

In 1891, the first public school in the Naruna area was established at the Pugh place. After several moves, a four-room school was built, and over the years, more rooms were added to create Naruna High School. In 1910, Miss Rosa Gilliam became principal, serving for 19 years. In this photograph of the 1936 graduating class, only Mildred Crabtree is identified (second row, second from right). (Courtesy of Virginia Crabtree Colbert.)

The Rustburg High School class of 1924 included, from left to right, Principal Page Morton, Mary Ethel Wright, Ruby Younger, Mary Herndon, Elizabeth Woodson, Mattie Keesee, Annie Dowdy, Dora Keesee, Dana Tweedy, Alyne Merryman, Mabel Green, and Maynard Clay. (Courtesy of Robert A. Caldwell.)

The Rustburg High School class of 1941 celebrates its 50-year reunion with some of the faculty. The faculty is in the first row, from left to right: Martha Turner, Elizabeth Moseley, and Edith Evans Trice. The graduates are behind, from left to right: Robert Watkins, Henry Almond, Jasper Fariss, and Frank L. Hege Jr. (Courtesy of Campbell County Historical Society.)

The Rustburg High School class of 1943 included, from left to right, (first row) Robert Winston, Clayton White, Clifton Phillips, Dennis Riddle, and Elwood Lair; (second row) Louise Wright, Kathleen Burnette, Gladys Tweedy, Thelma Shrader, Della Orndorff, Audrey Hardy, Doris S. Farmer, Elizabeth Neuffer, Blanche Williams, LaVorn Maddox, Eleanor Mason, and Rachel Wilkinson. Not pictured are Ann Merryman, Jim Swart, and Billy Fitch. (Courtesy of Gladys Tweedy Martin.)

The Rustburg High School class of 1949 included Jeanette Kreger, Barbara Blankenship, Joyce Pugh, Louise Driskill, Nancy Wooldridge, Doris Bobbitt, Martha Kabler, Mary Jane Wilmouth, Eugene Tweedy, Ronald Moon, Hunter Jones (teacher), James Ferguson, Elizabeth Stone, Mary Jane Torrence, Alma Dodson, Gordon Wright, and Richard Scott. (Courtesy of Elizabeth Stone Byers Potter.)

Before public schools for blacks were established, the first school for blacks in the area was conducted in this building, built around 1899, on the grounds of Pilot Mountain Baptist Church. The name comes from the mountain seen from the church, which is said to have served as a guide for Native Americans passing though the area. (Courtesy of Campbell County Historical Society.)

Concord High School is shown here in 1934, three years before it burned. An earlier building also burned, in 1911. The third Concord High School was built in 1938 and the last graduating class was in 1959. Since then, high school students have attended Rustburg High School. The Concord facility became an elementary school. (Courtesy of Gladys Tweedy Martin.)

The staff of *The Original*, the 1934 yearbook of Concord High School, posed for this photograph. The members included, in no particular order, Elizabeth Lee, Robert Feagans, Jack Martin, Maryon Tweedy, Charles Feagans, and Harold Caldwell. Instructors mentioned in the yearbook were Mr. Moore, Miss Whitlow, Mr. Campbell, Miss Scott, Miss Cross, Miss Cardwell, Miss Evans, and Miss Harvey. (Courtesy of Gladys Tweedy Martin.)

Gravel Ridge School, a one-room school on Red House Road, was in existence by 1880, making it one of the county's first schools. After a second room was added, the building was replaced around 1918 with a three-room school, which closed in 1944 and became the home economics cottage at Rustburg High School. The two-room school shown became a private residence. (Courtesy of the Campbell County Historical Society.)

When the Hat Creek School was demolished in the 1990s, it was over 100 years old. It began as a one-room school but grew into three rooms, holding grades one through nine. In 1932, eighth and ninth graders were bused to Naruna High School and in 1940, the entire school merged with Brookneal School. (Courtesy of Virginia Crabtree Colbert.)

All that is left of the Sherwill School on Route 606 are its foundations. It began as a two-room school and later, four grades were taught in one room with a single teacher. Once students went through the four grades, they were transferred to Concord Elementary for "higher education." The school closed in the mid-1930s, and the building was reportedly sold for the lumber. (Courtesy of Revely B. Carwile Jr.)

When a school ceased to be used for its original purpose, it was often sold at auction and moved to the buyer's property. The building then may have been used as a house or as an outbuilding on a farm. This poster shows the auction sale for a number of county schools. (Courtesy of Campbell County School Administration.)

PUBLIC AUCTION SALE
Of Schoolhouses and Lots
on the Respective School Premises

By virtue of authority vested in the undersigned by order of the Circuit Court of Campbell County, Virginia, entered at the March term, 1930, the following schoolhouses and lots will be offered for sale at public auction on the respective premises promptly at the time shown,

On Saturday, JULY 12th, 1930:

1. At 9:00 A. M. Providence 1-room schoolhouse and 1 acre of land on State Highway between Rustburg and Lynchburg, adjoining W. K. Balfagh and others.

2. At 10:00 A. M. Feagans 1-room white schoolhouse and lot containing 1 acre near Grace Church and Virginia U. S. Highway No. 60, adjoining C. B. Feagans and others.

3. At 10:30 A. M. Rode's 1-room schoolhouse and lot containing 1 acre on State Highway No. 43 between Rustburg and Concord Depot.

4. At 11:00 A. M. Woodland 1-room white schoolhouse and lot containing 1 acre on Wyatt Shop Public Road adjoining Wheeler and others.

5. At 12:00 M. Rockhouse 2-room white school and lot containing 2 acres on the Wilkerson Road some four miles east of Gladys.

6. At 12:30 P. M. Border 1-room white schoolhouse and lot containing 1 acre on old Brookneal and Rustburg Road, adjoining G. W. Rosser and others.

7. At 1:00 P. M. Edge 3-room schoolhouse and lot containing 4 acres on Collin's Ferry Road, adjoining D. P. Minix and others.

8. At 2:00 P. M. Island 1-room schoolhouse and lot containing 1 acre, adjoining Frank T. Francis and others, near the Gladys-Long Island Road.

9. At 3:00 P. M. Garbee 1-room schoolhouse and lot containing 1 acre near Lynchburg and Danville State Highway opposite T. E. Williams store, adjoining R. E. Garbee and others.

10. At 3:30 P. M. Lawyers 4-room schoolhouse and lot containing 3 acres, on west side of public road between the village and station, adjoining H. W. Brandt and others.

11. At 5:00 P. M. old colored school lot known as "Rabbit Hollow" near Altavista, containing 1 acre and being same conveyed to School Trustees of Otter River District by A. H. Moorman and wife.

TERMS: One-fourth cash, balance in 6, 12, and 18 months, equal payments, with interest, secured by first-lien deed of trust on the properties, with the privilege to purchasers to anticipate payments. Reasonable insurance required.

Manner of Sale: In each case the building, with the privilege of its removal for a period of 90 days and the lot on which it is located will be offered separately and then the respective school buildings and their lots will be offered as a whole. The buildings cannot be torn down or removed until fully paid for.

All sales subject to confirmation by the court.

These are public properties and everyone interested in buildings or materials is urged to come early and bid on them.

County School Board of Campbell County,
By J. J. Fray, Division Superintendent, Rustburg, Va.
PLEASE POST

Brown's School stands at the intersection of East Ferry Road and Mitchell's Mill Road on land given by the Brown family, originally of Hell Bend. This photograph from about 1925 includes children of Jackson Warren Moore and Lutie Brown. In the first row, Alec Moore, with the toy train, stands next to his sister, Gladys Brown Moore, holding her doll. In the third row in white hats are Ethel Martha Moore and Rachel Julia Moore. (Courtesy of Billie Newman Carwile.)

The annual art show is sponsored by the county's Department of Recreation. Schoolchildren, as well as adults, display their artistic endeavors for the public's viewing. The show gives young people an opportunity to have an audience beyond their school walls and is held on the Historic Courthouse Square. (Courtesy of Campbell County Historical Society.)

This Peakland School building in the northern portion of the county, now a private residence, is notable for its resemblance to the Alamo. It was sold in 1923, after it was replaced by a larger Peakland School building on Oak Lane, near Virginia Baptist Hospital. This community experienced rapid growth after the development of Rivermont and the extension of streetcars into Peakland before being annexed into Lynchburg in 1926. (Courtesy of Revely B. Carwile Jr.)

Eight

SCHOOL FAIR

The first school fair to be held in Virginia, sponsored by the Virginia Federation of Garden Clubs, was held at Rustburg in 1908. The fair was organized around the county schools, each of which proudly displayed its school banner in the parade. A separate fair was held for the African American schools. The excitement built as the participants assembled for a parade down Rustburg's main street. (Courtesy of Mr. and Mrs. Charles F. Jones.)

PROCESSION FORMING, CAMPBELL CO. SCHOOL FAIR
OCT. 1913, RUSTBURG, VA.

Fair leaders organize their groups to ensure an orderly procession in front of Rustburg High School, which housed both elementary and high school students. The Eagles, a band from nearby Lynchburg, prepared to lead the procession to the exhibit area around the courthouse and the school fair hall. Etta Brandt, former supervisor of instruction, recorded that the students and teachers marched to the court green to sing "My Country 'Tis of Thee." School banners were proudly waved to show school spirit. (Courtesy of Mr. and Mrs. Charles F. Jones.)

PART OF PROCESSION, CAMPBELL CO. SCHOOL FAIR
OCT. 17, 1913   RUSTBURG, VA.   J.P. BELL CO. INC.   #7

The fair parade marches on past Rust Meadows, the white house on the left, which is across from Rustburg Middle School and owned by Dr. Otis Watkins, a prominent Rustburg physician. His office was in a front room of the house, which patients entered through a separate sidewalk, which is still visible today. Many spectators came on the train from Lynchburg and Brookneal; one report estimated the number coming by rail to be 4,500 people. (Courtesy of Mr. and Mrs. Charles F. Jones.)

TALKING CROPS
CAMPBELL CO. SCHOOL FAIR, OCT 17, 1913, RUSTBURG VA.   J.P. BELL CO INC.

Local farmers discuss livestock prices and other matters pertaining to agriculture at the school fair. Before modern communications, events such as these were important means of exchanging information about crop yields, livestock prices, and weather conditions. The Boys' Corn Club was established by the United States Department of Agriculture to encourage knowledge and training in agricultural pursuits. The fair provided an opportunity for the contestants to demonstrate their expertise. (Courtesy of Mr. and Mrs. Charles F. Jones.)

POULTRY EXHIBIT

CAMPBELL CO. SCHOOL FAIR
OCT. 17, 1913, RUSTBURG VA.   J.P. BELL CO INC.

Campbell County ladies in fancy hats gathered around the poultry exhibits, where they saw a wide variety of hens and roosters, such as guinea fowl, Rhode Island Reds, White Leghorns, and Plymouth Rocks. Since there was no refrigeration at this time, serving fried chicken for a meal meant that someone went to the hen house shortly before mealtime. (Courtesy of Mr. and Mrs. Charles F. Jones.)

110

100 YD. DASH, CAMBELL CO. SCHOOL FAIR.
OCT.17,1913, RUSTBURG VA.
J.P. BELL CO. INC.

Young boys line up for the start of the 100-yard dash. Physical fitness was an important part of the lifestyle of the time. Young men and boys took great pride in demonstrating their physical attributes and prowess. One contestant appears to have an early start. (Courtesy of Mr. and Mrs. Charles F. Jones.)

100 YD. DASH, CAMPBELL CO. SCHOOL FAIR.
OCT. 17, 1913 - RUSTBURG VA.
J.P. BELL CO. INC.

Young runners are off in a cloud of dust as the crowd cheers from the balcony of the old Fountain Hotel and from the street. One overzealous young lad has already taken a tumble in what appears to have been a very close race. (Courtesy of Mr. and Mrs. Charles F. Jones.)

AWARD OF PRIZES, CAMPBELL CO. SCHOOL FAIR
OCT. 7, 1913. RUSTBURG VA

The school fair, held in the School Fair Hall in Rustburg from 1908–1916, provided an opportunity for students to exhibit their best work. Prizes were awarded in art, literary works, agriculture, horticulture, domestic science, and industrial art. Competition was fierce since winning a blue ribbon was an honor discussed for years. Getting an award at the school fair brought a great deal of recognition for the young competitors. The spelling bee was an equally spirited event with one competitor from each school. (Courtesy of Mr. and Mrs. Charles F. Jones.)

ONE MILE RACE
CAMPBELL CO. SCHOOL FAIR, RUSTBURG VA.
OCT. 17, 1913

This view shows the corner location of Stanley Perrow's General Merchandise Store. This building was later replaced by a brick store. To the immediate right is a section of the Fountain Hotel, which was torn down to make space for the Miles Brothers Hardware Store. Only the central portion of the Fountain Hotel remains today. (Courtesy of Mr. and Mrs. Charles F. Jones.)

112

SCHOOL FAIR BLDG.
RUSTBURG, VA.

J.P. BELL CO. INC.

At this time, the Commonwealth of Virginia was placing an emphasis on improving agricultural methods, as well as public education. Campbell was the first county in Virginia to initiate a school fair. The fair hall was used for meetings, concerts, exhibitions, and athletic events. It also served as the town's high school gymnasium. Both the black and white communities made extensive use of the facility. The School Fair Hall, completed in 1909, was located adjacent to the old courthouse in what later became the parking lot for the hardware store. The building burned in 1917, and school fairs were discontinued in Rustburg. However, an agricultural and school fair was held in Altavista in 1926. This fair was open to men, women, and children. Later, the farm show in Lynchburg became the "show ground" for agricultural and domestic entries. (Courtesy of Mr. and Mrs. Charles F. Jones.)

This view of the busy street in front of the courthouse and some of the first automobiles foretells the dramatic changes about to occur in transportation. Almost all the spectators shown here grew up in the horse-and-buggy era. They would have patronized the livery stables, tack shops, and tan yards, all of which were located in the vicinity of the courthouse. The 1909 Report of the Campbell County Teachers Association stated in reference to the school fair: "This is one of the most successful ways we have found for arousing the interest of the people, for when they come in crowds as they do to see this fair, they see for themselves what can and is being done by their children and they are more aroused for the cause of education afterwards." (Courtesy of Mr. and Mrs. Charles F. Jones.)

Nine

TRANSPORTATION

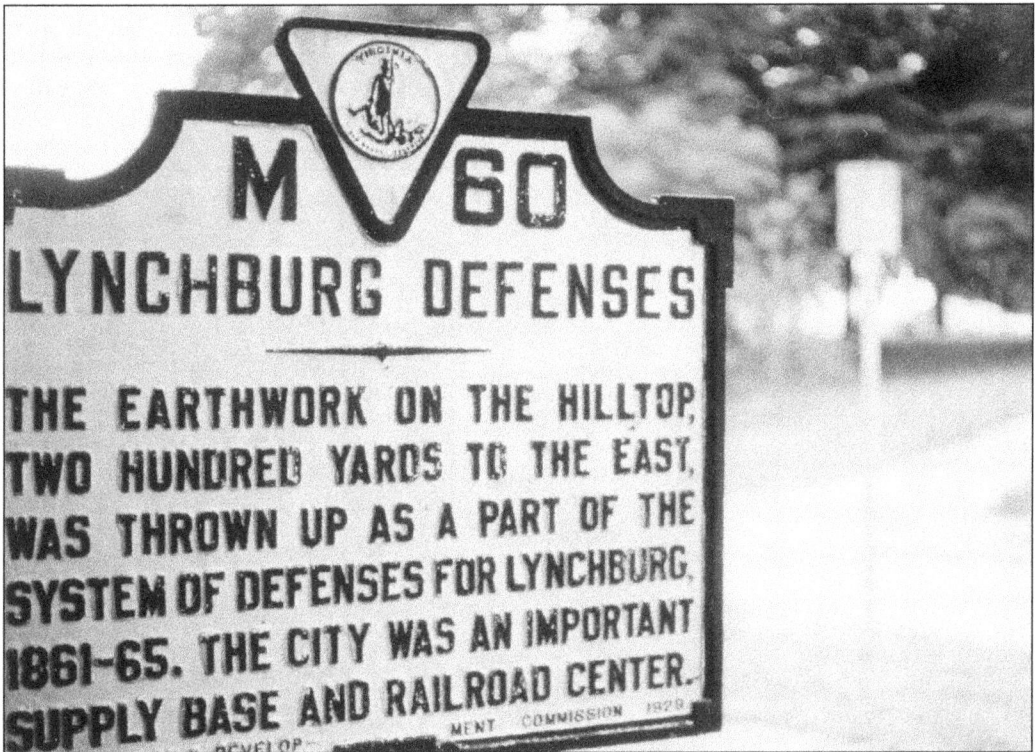

A Confederate redoubt was constructed in 1864–1865 at the hilltop where Routes 501 and 460 intersect, protecting Campbell Courthouse Road, Concord Turnpike, and approaches to Lynchburg and the James River Kanawha Canal. This fort was demolished during highway cloverleaf construction. Earlier redoubts in Campbell County, Fort Early, and Fort McCausland were scenes of fighting on June 17–18, 1864, during the Battle of Lynchburg, and were annexed into Lynchburg in 1926. (Courtesy of Revely B. Carwile Jr. and Douglas K. Harvey.)

This depot in Concord was a replacement for the one burned by General Hunter in his raid on the area. The Union general destroyed the depot, the commissary, and a train, but no other buildings in Concord. It is said that the stationmaster's house was spared because someone told General Hunter that a woman and children were in the building. At that time, Hunter was called back to Fort Early in Lynchburg, so Concord was as far east as his raid extended. (Courtesy of Campbell County Historical Society.)

The Southern Railway depot in Altavista was built in 1909, the same year as the Virginian Railway station. Prior to the completion of the depot, two boxcars served duty at the station, which burned in 1936. It was replaced by a brick structure, which now serves as the Altavista Chamber of Commerce building. (Courtesy of Robert B. Carpenter, Jr.)

Before Six Mile Bridge No. 58, east of Lynchburg, was completed, rail passengers were transferred to canal boats for the remainder of their journey to Lynchburg. The bridge was completed around 1853, but in 1865, the Confederates burned it to deter the Yankees. The bridge was rebuilt in 1866 and used by several railway companies for more than a century, finally stopping in 1972. (Courtesy of Mary Walker Gough.)

When Norfolk & Western laid its rail line through Campbell County, trestles such as this one on Eastbrook Road at Beaver Creek had to be erected. This trestle was said to be the highest curved trestle in Virginia at the time it was built in 1907. The trestle has only one track but was built to accommodate a second track. (Courtesy of Elizabeth Gough Sollenberger.)

When Norfolk & Western Railroad was putting in its rail line, the surveyors slept in available housing, and the Chinese and Italian workers set up camps. This scene is of the engineers using a home on the Glover L. Gough farm around 1907. Remains of the Italian camp have been found on the property. (Courtesy of Thomas E. Gough.)

This bridge over the Norfolk & Western beltline tracks near Eastbrook Road was built around 1907. The hump in the center of the bridge was an afterthought, created out of necessity to provide clearance after a railroad crane snagged the bridge. The bridge was dismantled and rebuilt with a hump to add more clearance. The bridge was replaced around 1991. (Courtesy Campbell County Historical Society.)

This Virginian Railway passenger locomotive is in Altavista. The Virginian passenger trains usually consisted of the locomotive, a railway post office car, and two passenger cars. The line transported passengers boarding in Altavista to points eastward to Norfolk. Passenger service was discontinued in 1957. (Courtesy of Robert B. Carpenter Jr.)

Around 1873, railroad workers laid brick to line the tunnel arch beneath what now is Rivermont Avenue, from the area of Riverside Park to manufacturing lots along Bedford Avenue and Lexington Turnpike (Hollins Mill Road). This Norfolk Southern line remains in operation. Piedmont automobiles were manufactured a few hundred yards to the south of this location. This portion of the county was annexed into Lynchburg in 1926. (Courtesy of Revely B. Carwile Jr.)

This American Big Winner No. 31 grader was built around 1880 by American Road Machinery Co. in Kennett Square, Pennsylvania. As a horse-drawn grader, it was pulled by a team of four or more horses and was used to build early roads that eventually became our county roads. The refurbished grader is on display at Lynchburg's public works complex on Memorial Avenue. (Courtesy of Thomas E. Gough.)

It is easy for us to forget that some of the highways we use today were built with manual labor and simple machines. In the 1920s, Ernest (left) and Glover Tweedy use a tractor, a Model A truck, and a boom to create a highway in the Rustburg area near Beaver Creek. Today, that highway is four lanes in some sections. (Courtesy of Richard Blanks.)

Campbell County Judge Frank Nelson (front seat passenger) and his son, Page (driver), are shown here in a Maxwell car. An invoice for a Maxwell sold to Judge Nelson in 1911 by Bolton and Bowles of Lynchburg reflects the cost of $650 for a "Model T Maxwell Car and Equipment." Judge Nelson owned two Maxwell automobiles. (Courtesy of John D. Nelson.)

This Model T Ford, known as "Old Ironsides," belonged to Martha Evans, a teacher at Concord High School. Miss Evans was a beloved county educator who is said to have been the first female in Concord to drive a car. She taught at Concord for 51 years, retiring in 1945. (Courtesy of Gladys Tweedy Martin.)

Before its destruction, the Marysville Bridge was the second-oldest standing covered bridge in the state. This bridge replaced one that was destroyed, along with many other bridges in the county, in a flood in 1878. It was used until 1952, when Route 705 was rebuilt with a modern bridge. Plans to demolish the bridge met with outcries from the citizens, so the county's Board of Supervisors agreed to allow it to continue standing as a "monument to the past." The bridge withstood the ravages of vandals as well as the ravages of time, but finally fell on September 6, 1996, to the wrath of Hurricane Fran. The covering on bridges provided protection from the elements for the floor and under-structure, a respite from rain for travelers, and a private spot for courting couples. (Courtesy of Robert A. Caldwell.)

Mansion Truss Bridge, built around 1912, spanned the Staunton River into Pittsylvania County on Route 640 east of Altavista. The one-lane bridge replaced an earlier covered bridge and was named for the mansion of Maj. John Ward (1712–1816). The bridge, which was on the Virginia Landmarks Register and in the National Register of Historic Places, was replaced by a wider bridge in the late 1990s. (Courtesy of Robert A. Caldwell.)

The Staunton River has two names. At its origin and at its ending, it is called the Roanoke, but from its mouth at Back Creek to its confluence with the Dan River, it is often called the Staunton. The Battle of Staunton River Bridge near Randolph was fought on June 25, 1864, when, as Herman Ginther described, a "small band of old men and boys fought off a vastly superior Federal force." This replacement bridge was built over the Staunton River between Brookneal and Halifax County. (Courtesy of Willie Hodges Booth Museum of the Staunton River Historical Society.)

The Old Fort Airport was built in 1946 by Warren Falwell. Named for the nearby Confederate fort, Falwell changed the name to Falwell Airport in the early 1970s, when the fort was removed for highway construction. From the time he was a child, Campbell County businessman Calvin Falwell, Warren's son, had an interest in aviation, achieving his first solo flight on July 17, 1944. Two years later, he became a dealer for Ercoupes, and on December 26, 1946, piloted an Ercoupe N93462 to the first plane landing at the Old Fort Airport. His brother, Lawrence, also took up flying, and together they operated Falwell Airport, which is still in business today. Both Falwell brothers were inducted into the Virginia Aviation Hall of Fame. (Courtesy of Edna "Pee Wee" Falwell Twiddy.)

Today's Falwell Airport is a fixed base operation, offering flying instructions, rental planes, and airplane maintenance. The runway, which runs east to west, resembles a ski slope. Edna "Pee Wee" Falwell Twiddy describes it in this manner: "Planes take off from the western end headed east, and by the time the runway goes downhill, the plane is airborne. For landing, the planes approach the east end of the runway headed west, touching down on the bottom and coasting uphill." This 2010 view shows the airport, as well as the Truck Body Company, on the northern side of Route 460. Truck Body Corporation, as it was known then, was formed by Calvin and Lawrence Falwell in 1947, and at that time, was located on Campbell Avenue. Later, a new facility was built on Richmond Highway and was sold in 2006. (Courtesy of Falwell Aviation.)

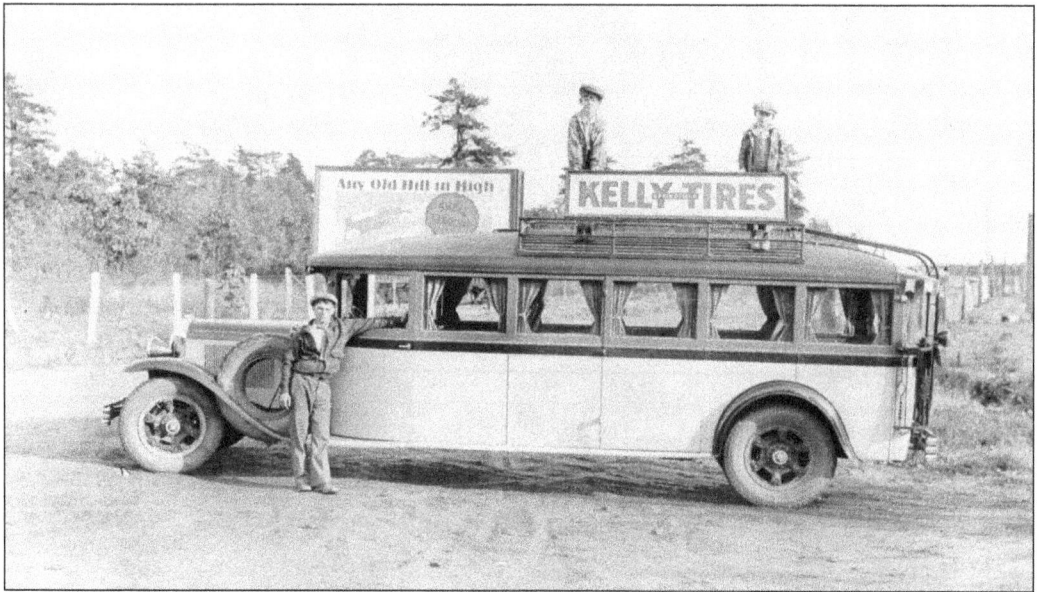

Local businessman Warren Falwell recognized a need for public transportation for residents of the rural areas in the county. In 1929, he established Southern Passenger Motor Lines, Inc. The buses were Buick cars converted to 17-passenger buses. Falwell also owned several Mack and White buses. The bus route extended all the way to Richmond and North Carolina. Falwell eventually sold his Virginia bus route to Greyhound in 1934 and his North Carolina route to Trailways in 1936. (Courtesy of Edna "Pee Wee" Falwell Twiddy.)

Warren Falwell, at the time of this photograph, owned two wreckers. One of them, a long-boom wrecker, was the largest in the area. In her book about her father, C. *Warren Falwell: Entrepreneur & Family Man*, Edna "Pee Wee" Falwell Twiddy tells of the wrecker being used to move a desk and safe from the second floor office of Judge Burks. The judge closed off the street to accommodate the transport. (Courtesy of Edna "Pee Wee" Falwell Twiddy.)

BIBLIOGRAPHY

A *Guide to Campbell County*. Rustburg, VA: County of Campbell, Office of the County Administrator, 2010.

"A Historical Study of Education in Campbell County, 1782–1940." University of Virginia Thesis of Mary Etta Brandt, 1941.

Campbell County, Virginia Heritage Book. Campbell County, VA: The Heritage Book Committee, 2003.

Carpenter, Robert B. Jr. *A Pictorial History of Altavista, Virginia, 1907–2007*. Altavista, VA: self-published, 2007.

Early, R.H. *Campbell Chronicles and Family Sketches: Embracing the History of Campbell County, Virginia, 1782–1926*. Lynchburg, VA: J.P. Bell Company, 1927.

Edwards, Pauline H. *The New Campbell County Chronicles*. Altavista, VA: Altavista Printing Company Inc., 1981.

Ginther, Herman. *Captain Staunton's River*. Richmond, VA: The Dietz Press Inc., 1968.

Lest It Be Forgotten: A Scrapbook of Campbell County. The Historical Committee of the Bicentennial Commission of Campbell County, Virginia. Altavista, VA: Altavista Printing Company Inc., 1976.

Popek, Diane. *Tracks Along the Staunton: A History of Leesville, Lynch Station, Hurt, and Altavista*. Amherst, VA: Central Virginia Printing Inc., 1984.

Visit us at
arcadiapublishing.com